Spot the DINOSAUR on the Island

Stella Maidment

Illustrated by
Joelle Dreidemy

QED

Pterosaurs

Plant eaters

Eggs

Velociraptor

Plesiosaurus

This baby Tyrannosaurus Rex (*Tie-ran-uh-sore-us Rex*), or T. Rex for short, is hiding inside the book. Can you find him in every scene?

The Supersaurus
(*Super-sore-us*)
was one of the
biggest dinosaurs.

It was as long as ten
elephants standing
in a line!

Can you spot these things?

red lizard palm tree cactus feather bones

The Velociraptor's (*Vell-oss-ee-rap-tor's*) name means 'speedy robber'. This little dinosaur could run very fast.

All baby
dinosaurs started
life by hatching out
of eggs – even the
really big ones!

Although some dinosaurs ate meat, most of them were plant eaters.

Can you spot these things?

red fish   fern   pine cone   blue flower   snake

The Triceratops
(*Try-serra-tops*) had
a big frill around its
head and three horns to
protect it from enemies.

Can you spot these dinosaurs?

Troodon
(*Troh-oh-don*)

Allosaurus
(*Al-oh-sore-us*)

Dracorex
(*Dray-ko-rex*)

Gastonia
(*Gas-toe-nee-ah*)

Oviraptor
(*Oh-vee-rap-tor*)

How many spikes are there at the end of my tail?

The Stegosaurus (*Steg-uh-sore-us*) had huge, bony plates along its back and spikes on its tail that were as long as swords!

Can you spot these things?

green lizard   white flower   fish   yellow dinosaur   eggshell

The Pterosaurs (*Terra-sores*) flew in the sky above the dinosaurs. Some of them were as big as planes!

The Plesiosaurus
(*Plez-io-sore-us*) lived in
the sea. It had a long neck,
four flippers and sharp teeth.

Can you spot these things?

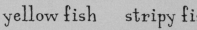

yellow fish   stripy fish   green shell   turtle   squid

Can you spot these things?

hammer · biscuits · brush · dinosaur tooth · camera

Did you Know?

Of course, Dinosaur Island isn't a real place. In fact, lots of these dinosaurs lived millions of years apart and so they would never have met.

Some of the dinosaurs' closest relatives are still around today. You might see one if you look out of your window. They're birds!

No one is certain what colour dinosaurs were, but we know that some had feathers and most of them had scaly skin.

One of the biggest dinosaurs that we know about is the gigantic Argentinosaurus (Ar-gen-teen-oh-sore-us). Maybe someone will discover an even bigger one soon!

Anyone can look for dinosaur fossils. One of the first fossil hunters was a little girl called Mary Anning, who lived in England about 200 years ago.

More dinosaur fun!

Make a dino-land

Collect little stones and arrange them on an old tray. Use sand if you have some. Fill a jar lid with water for a pond and use twigs for trees. Add some toy dinosaurs, or you could make your own.

Make a baby dinosaur

Carefully decorate half of an empty clean eggshell with felt-tip pens. Make a dinosaur head and neck out of modelling clay; use lots of colours. Mark the eyes and mouth with a pencil. Fix the dinosaur inside the shell so that its face is peeping out.

Hide and seek

Choose a cuddly toy that you can hide around your home for a friend or family member to spot, just like the T. Rex in the book! You could hide other objects and make a list of things to find.

Do the dinosaur stomp!

Take two empty tissue boxes. Stick tape across each hole so they fit your feet. Paint the boxes or glue on pieces of coloured paper. Ask an adult to help you cut out triangular 'claws' from a washing-up sponge and glue them on. Put on your feet and stomp!

Designer: Krina Patel
Editor: Tasha Percy
Editorial Director: Victoria Garrard
Art Director: Laura Roberts-Jensen

Copyright © QED Publishing 2014

First published in the UK in 2014 by
QED Publishing
Part of The Quarto Group
The Old Brewery,
6 Blundell Street,
London, N7 9BH

www.qed-publishing.co.uk

A catalogue record for this book is available from the British Library.

ISBN 978 1 78171 653 3

Printed in China